CHANDNI CHHILLAR

Unscripted LIFE

A Memoir of Love, Loss, and the Time We Take for Granted

BlueRose ONE .com
Stories Matter
NewDelhi • London

BLUEROSE PUBLISHERS
India | U.K.

BlueRose ONE
Stories Matter
NewDelhi • London

For permissions requests or inquiries regarding this publication, please contact:

BLUEROSE PUBLISHERS
www.BlueRoseONE.com
info@bluerosepublishers.com
+91 8882 898 898
+4407342408967

ISBN: 978-93-7542-202-0

Cover Design: Shivam Gaur
Typesetting: Sagar

First Edition: March 2026

Unscripted Life

A Harsh Reality No One Is Ever Ready to Accept

We have all heard of scripted movies—stories carefully planned, dialogues rehearsed, endings neatly tied. Sometimes, we even try to "script" our own lives, imagining that we can control every step, every choice. How foolish we are to think this way.

Life is unscripted. Our story is already written by God, and not even a blink happens solely by our choice. No matter how much we plan, no matter how much we wish, life unfolds on its own terms. Every story in this world is unscripted, and ours is no exception.

This truth is painful, but necessary to face. Whatever time we are given, that time is precious—and it is meant to be spent with the people we love. Yet we, stubborn and blind, run after money, success, growth, and status, never satisfied with what we have. In the process, we ignore our parents, siblings, and friends. We forget that giving even thirty minutes a day to them could make a world of difference.

We never consider the moment when they will no longer be here. And when that moment comes, all we can do is cry and regret the words unsaid, the hugs missed, the love left unexpressed. We wish desperately for just a little more time—a little more time to tell them how much they mean to us.

I chose the name *Unscripted Life* for this book in remembrance of my father. His life, like all of ours, was unpredictable, unscripted, and filled with moments that no planning could prepare him—or us—for. This book is my way of honoring him, reflecting on the lessons his life taught me, and cherishing the time we have with the ones we love before it slips away.

Prologue

Before the Story Begins

Some stories are not meant to be written. They live quietly in the heart, hidden behind smiles, routines, and every day strength. This story forced its way out of me—not because I wanted to relive the pain, but because I was afraid of forgetting the details.

I am writing this not as a writer, but as a daughter who lost her anchor. This book is not about death—it is about love, patience, sacrifice, and a man who lived his entire life for others. If you find yourself reflected in these pages, pause call your parents, Sit with them. Listen to their stories while you still can.

Life is unscripted. And sometimes, it takes everything from us to teach us that truth.

Introduction

Life Story of the Most Patient Man I Have Ever Known

This is the life story of the most patient person I have ever met in my life—my Papa.

A few years ago, I used to think of myself as patient. I would say, *"I don't get mad easily."* But as I grew older, I realized that in front of him, I didn't even stand a chance. My family often says I am his replica—like father, like daughter. And perhaps that is true.

He always believed that whatever happens, happens for a good reason. He taught me that we cannot change what is already written. He believed in doing good, no matter how others treated him—no matter if someone did wrong or tried to harm him. His philosophy was simple: whatever people do will come back to them in their own time; there is no need for us to respond with negativity.

I truly believe that because of his good deeds, he is in heaven today. If I ever hope to be like him, it will take me a lifetime to achieve even ten percent of what he was. And yet, I keep trying. I want to carry his qualities, to embody all the versions of him. Because no matter which version of himself he was at any moment, he never hurt anyone. He never spoke harshly or caused pain.

Of course, he had his weaknesses, as we all do. But he managed his life so gracefully that no one could ever point them out. Even if mistakes happened unknowingly, he lived in a way that commanded respect and love. At the end of the day, we are all human—and even superheroes have their flaws. The measure of a person is not in perfection, but in how they live despite their imperfections.

This book is my tribute to my father—my way of honoring his life, his lessons, and his incredible patience. It is my way of keeping him alive through words, memories, and the love that will never fade.

Contents

Chapter 1

A Childhood That Ended Too Soon

He was only eleven—perhaps twelve—when childhood quietly left him. Not with noise or warning, but with responsibility. At an age when most children are still learning what they like and dislike, he was already learning what survival meant.

Although he had a mother, brothers, and sisters, the reality of the 1990s was unforgiving. Mothers did not usually work then, and dependence was not a choice—it was a limitation. So the weight fell on him. He worked wherever he could, take on multiple jobs, carrying burdens that were never meant for a boy his age.

When he was recruited into the army, two contrasting phases of his life began at once. On one hand, there was stability, discipline, and honor. On the other, the responsibilities never stopped growing. Life didn't pause to let him breathe. It simply demanded more.

Even within his own family, support leaned toward the elder siblings. His mother favored them, knowingly or unknowingly, but he never questioned it. He never raised his voice in complaint, never criticized, and never asked why. Silence became his strength and acceptance his armor.

His childhood was not difficult in the ordinary sense—it was filled with real struggle-the kind that reshapes a person from the inside. He did not get the opportunity to study properly, because long before books, he was studying responsibility. While others learned lessons from classrooms, he learned them from hunger, duty, and sacrifice.

There was no teenage phase for him. No time to be reckless, care free, or young. While others were discovering themselves, he was holding everything together. He faced problems that most adults would find overwhelming, and he faced them alone.

When I try to imagine living a life like his, I fail. I don't think I would have been strong enough. I might have broken. I might have given up. But he didn't. He kept moving forward—quietly, relentlessly—struggling every single day, not for himself alone, but for the promise of a better future for those who came after him.

Chapter 2

Married Life of My Father

Marriage is not just a union of two people; it is a responsibility that reshapes an entire life. When a person is still in their teenage years, the heart longs to enjoy youth, freedom, and simple happiness. One is not prepared for the weight of marriage or the expectations that come with it. But life does not always wait for readiness.

He was married young—to a girl he had never seen, never spoken to, never met. That was how things were then. And that is how my mother entered his life, marking the beginning of a new journey for both of them.

He was serving in the defense, which meant he could never stay beside his wife for long. Duty called him away repeatedly and apart from regular duty he was playing boxing. At home, he carried the responsibilities of being a son, a brother, and a husband. Beyond the walls of home, standing at the borders, he was a soldier—protecting his country. Two worlds rested on his shoulders, yet he never complained about either.

While he stood guard at the borders, my mother was learning to settle into a new family, a new home, and a completely new life. She too, carried her share of silence with grace. No matter how unhappy she might have been at times, for whatever reason, she never spoke a single word against his family—not to him, not to neighbor's, not to anyone. She was and remains, a true family woman.

Married life soon brought children into their world. On the 10th of January 1990, my sister entered their lives. That day, my father was filled with a happiness that words cannot fully describe. He was the kind of man for whom sons and daughters were equal. To him, a child was a blessing, not a preference. And she was their first.

For some time, my father managed to keep my mother with him in Ahmadabad and later in Dehradun. Life was never easy—his means were limited, his schedule uncertain—but he still tried his best to give her comfort and happiness. For him, family always came first. He gave more than he could afford, both emotionally and materially, because providing for his loved ones was never a burden—it was his purpose.

In Ahmadabad, my mother lived alone in the army quarters. Seeing this, my father's friends stepped in with quiet kindness.

They requested a change in quarters so that their wives and my mother could live closer together. It was a small gesture, but it meant that my mother was no longer alone.

On weekends, my father and mother found joy in simple moments. He used to play badminton with her, take her out for shopping, and spend whatever little time he had making her feel cared for. He always wanted to give my mother a life of comfort —even luxury—despite the limitations of his circumstances.

He never liked my mother traveling alone. Not because he doubted her strength, but because he wanted her to travel with him, surrounded by comfort and safety. He wanted to be there— to ensure that every journey was easy for her, just as he tried to make life easy in every other way he knew how.

These were not grand gestures the world noticed. But they were quiet acts of love that defined who he was.

A few years later, my brother was born—their first son. My grandmother adored him deeply. In those days, sons were often valued more than daughters. Girls were seen as a responsibility, while boys were placed on a pedestal. That was the reality of that era.

My grandmother wanted to spoil my brother, almost to the point where it could have created problems for my parents. But my mother and father stood firm .With patience, discipline, and love; they raised him with good values. No matter how much affection surrounded him, he never became spoiled. *Touchwood*, he grew up with manners, respect, and balance—because my parents ensured that love never turned into entitlement.

Their parenting spoke louder than traditions. They chose values over favoritism and upbringing over indulgence.

Yet my father remained unchanged. His love never divided. His responsibilities only grew—but so did his strength.

Then I came into their lives.

I was born early in the morning, though I never became an early bird. I was born on 1st January 1998. Everyone in the family joked that my father had won a lottery of one lakh—because in those days, people believed that with that amount, you could easily marry off a girl.

My grandmother never liked me much, mainly because of my dark skin tone but my father never cared—not even for a second. He loved me with his whole heart.

Once, when he was home on leave from the army, I fell sick. I was only a few months old. I kept crying nonstop, and he held me in his arms the entire night, comforting me. He didn't sleep at all, yet he never complained. Not once.

Another time, while playing at home, I hit my toe on a nail. He immediately dropped everything; picked me up in his arms, and took me to the village doctor for first aid. After that, he made me sit on his shoulders, bought me a toffee, and kept telling me softly, *"It's going to be okay soon, beta."*

Every father would do this, people say. May be.

But what made him different was this—he never got angry at me. Not once.

He gave me freedom from the very day I was born. Freedom to move, to fall, to learn, and to grow—always knowing that no matter what happened, his arms would be there to catch me

Chapter 3

A Father Before Anything Else

Becoming a father did not change my father—it revealed who he truly was.

By the time he held his children in his arms, responsibility was already an old companion. Yet fatherhood added a new layer to his life: one filled with quiet joy, deeper sacrifice, and unconditional love. Whether it was a daughter or a son, it never made a difference to him. A child was a blessing, and he treated it as such.

His armed duty in the defense often kept him far from home. He missed birthdays, first steps, and first words—countless moments that never return. Yet even in his absence, his presence was always felt. His love traveled through letters, phone calls, and quiet reassurances to my mother—that no matter where he was posted, his family always came first.

After retiring from the armed forces and joining SBI Bank, life finally gave him what duty had taken away—time with us. He got the chance to celebrate birthdays, festivals, and family functions together. From then on, I never celebrated a birthday without him.

Most of the time, he was working on my birthday, yet he never failed to bring a cake and new clothes for me. Every year, his gift was the same—a watch. They were never from expensive brands, but they were priceless to me. I have always loved wearing watches, and he knew it.

He would say, "The whole family is there with you. Why didn't you cut the cake?" And I would stubbornly reply, "Aapke bina cake cut nahi karungi main. Mera cake aap hi cut karaoge." He would laugh and call me his "pagal beta."

As I grew older, I started celebrating my birthdays with friends too—fancy restaurants, laughter, photographs. But honestly, those birthdays with him were the best ones.

On Diwali, during Lakshmi pooja, I would sit close to him while he counted the money so I could ask for my share. After seeing the cash, I would say, *"Papa, yeh paise dedo na. Aapke paas toh bahut paise hain."* And he would smile and say, *"Sab tera hi toh hai."* I would reply, *"Mujhe sab nahi chahiye,bas 2000–3000 de do.Mujhe zyada laalach nahi hai."* He would laugh and say how easily his beta agreed.

Those were the moments that made life feel complete.

And now, from here onwards, I don't have anyone to ask for anything on my favorite occasions.

No birthdays, no festivals, no functions will ever feel the same. This absence will haunt me.

I was always excited about my birthdays. From December onwards, I would start demanding things from him—reminding him every single day that my birthday was coming. Every day, the demand would change depending on my mood. And he never said no. Whatever I asked for, his answer was always yes.

That was his love—quiet, unconditional, and endless.

At home, my mother became both parents in one. She carried the household, raised the children, and protected our innocence, all while waiting for a husband who served the nation before himself. She never complained. She never questioned fate. Together, they formed a partnership built not on comfort, but on understanding.

Whenever my father came home on leave, he tried to give us an entire lifetime of love in a few short days. Those moments were simple, yet priceless. He taught us values not through words, but through his actions—discipline, honesty, respect, and resilience. He didn't lecture us about life; he lived the example.

Money was never abundant, but dignity always was. He ensured that our needs were met, even if it meant denying his own. His dreams were quietly sacrificed so ours could breathe freely. He never announced his struggles, never demanded recognition. He simply carried on.

Watching him, I often wonder how someone who lost his own childhood so early managed to give us one filled with security. How a man who never had time to dream still built dreams for his children. I know I could never walk the path he walked. I would have stumbled long before the journey truly began.

But he stood firm—day after day, year after year—being a soldier at the border and a father in his heart. And in doing so, he became more than just a parent. He became the foundation of everything we are.

Chapter 4

The Sacrifices No One Saw

Some sacrifices are loud and visible. Others happen quietly, without witnesses, applause, or recognition. My father's sacrifices belonged to the second kind.

Every posting meant starting life again—new places, unfamiliar face, and long separations from his family. He learned to live with absence as a habit. While others returned home at the end of the day, he slept under unfamiliar skies, guarding borders most people would never see, protecting a country that would never know his name.

He carried two kinds of fatigue: the physical exhaustion of duty and the emotional weight of distance. Yet he never allowed either to harden him. He never came home bitter. He never let his struggles spill into our lives. Whatever pain he carried, he carried alone.

There were moments when life tested him relentlessly—financial pressure, family expectations, and the unspoken responsibility of being the one who never fail. Still, he chose silence over complaint. Strength, for him, was not about being loud; it was about enduring.

He wore the same calm face whether life was kind or cruel. Even when he was overlooked, even when his efforts went unnoticed, he continued. Not because it was easy, but because quitting was never an option he allowed himself.

What the world never saw was how much he gave up—his comfort, his youth, his rest, and sometimes his own happiness. He postponed his needs indefinitely, convincing himself that there would be time later. That time rarely came.

And yet, there was no resentment in him. Only acceptance. Only duty. Only love.

As his child, I now understand that the life I was able to live— the safety, the stability, the freedom—was built on sacrifices I was too young to see. Things I took for granted were paid for by his silent endurance.

If strength had a face, it would look like him. Quiet. Steady. Unbreakable.

Chapter 5

Across Oceans, Under His Wings

All three of us siblings went to the same school- Shri Rama Bharti Public School. I joined that school in second grade and stayed there until twelfth—one place, one uniform, one long journey of growing up.

In my school, girls were supposed to wear skirts but my father always sent me in pants. He wanted me to be comfortable in my own skin and my own clothes. The school principal didn't like it at all. Complaints came often. But my father never cared.

Whenever the school called him, the owner and staff would suddenly become nervous. Some would even avoid him, because they knew one thing very clearly—my father would speak logically, and he would never agree to something that was wrong. He never shouted never insulted, never created drama. He simply spoke the truth, and that was enough.

When I scored low marks, he never scolded me. He never said I wasn't studying properly. Instead, he questioned the teachers —why they weren't teaching properly. That was his way of protecting me. He believed that children should be guided, not pressured.

When I entered eleventh grade, my brother suggested that I take Arts because I wasn't very interested in studies. But I was stubborn. I told him, *"You took Commerce, so I will also take Commerce."* And that's exactly what I did.

The same thing happened again when I went to college. My brother suggested B.A., but once again I chose B.Com—not because it was easy, but because I wanted to prove something to myself. And my father supported me every time. He never forced his opinion on me. He always let me choose what I felt was right for me.

During college, I wanted to join the armed forces. Without hesitation, he allowed me to join NCC. Later, I prepared for CDS.

I never succeeded in joining the armed forces, but he never let my dream die. He never said, *"Enough now"* He never made me feel like a failure. Even when I missed the opportunity to join the Army—mostly because of my own negligence—he stood beside me, not disappointed, not angry.

The same freedom was given to my siblings. He never restricted education. He never said, *"You're a girl, you don't need to study so much."* In fact, being a girl, I was the one who went to a hostel for graduation. Later, I stayed in Delhi all by myself. He trusted me completely.

When I started working in an MNC, he suggested something unexpected. He said, *"If you want to work in private companies, why don't you go to Canada?"*

Honestly, I didn't like the idea at all.

I was living in my comfort zone—friends around me, a familiar routine, a life full of fun and ease. I didn't want to leave that. But he wanted me to enjoy life and build my future together. After a lot of hesitation, I agreed.

In my family I became the first girl to go abroad.

From paperwork to motivation, from doubts to fears—he was with me through the entire process of going to Canada. He constantly pushed me to live a better life, even when I wasn't ready for it.

The day my flight finally came, my heart was pounding. I was scared and excited at the same time. Before I left, he told me something he always used to say:

"Focus on your work. Study hard. Eat properly. Don't look at others and spend your money. Look at your own house first, then spend."

For the first few days in Canada, I was upset. I didn't like it. I struggled silently. I kept telling him that I wanted to come back. Honestly, I never liked Canada. Even while living there, my heart stayed back home.

But today, when I look back, I understand something I didn't see then.

He helped me build a future—quietly, patiently—without ever making me realize it. Because he was always there, I kept choosing comfort over growth. But his decision pushed me toward independence, strength, and stability.

Along the way, my friends and my brother helped me grab opportunities, learn new things, and stand on my own feet. But it was my father who opened the door.

Now that he is no more, I realize how far his vision reached—even when mine couldn't.

I wanted comfort. He wanted a future.

And somehow, because of him, I have both.

Chapter 6

3rd December—The Day My World Stopped

The third of December is the worst day of my life—a day I was never prepared for, not even in my dreams. And the truth is, no one is ever ready for a day like this.

That morning began like any other. I woke up, went to the gym, and carried a happiness I hadn't felt in a long time. January was close. I had booked my tickets to India for the 2nd of January so I could celebrate my birthday with my family. My birthday is on the1st of January, but due to certain reasons, I was arriving a day later. Still, I was excited—overwhelmingly excited.

As I got ready for work, my heart felt light. There were butterflies in my stomach, the good kind. At work, I told my colleagues that I was going to India. One of them smiled and said, *"You're spoiled by your dad's love. Finally, you're going to meet him after so long."* Everyone could see how happy I was that day. I was glowing with anticipation.

When it was time for lunch, I took my break earlier than usual. I couldn't focus on work anymore—I was too excited. I heated my food, set up my phone to watch a web series, and had just taken my first bite when my phone rang.

It was my brother.

He said he was coming to pick me up from work.

I was shocked. I asked him why. He didn't answer at first. I forced him to tell me what had happened. Then he said, *"Mom called.*

Dad is not responding."

In that moment, my entire life flipped. Everything collapsed within seconds. My heart refused to accept the reality of what I was hearing. I booked an Uber immediately and ran towards home, crying the entire way—crying with the hope that I would receive a call saying everything was okay, that my dad was fine.

I called my mom. My sister-in-law picked up instead. I asked her to give the phone to my mother. When I saw her crying, my whole world shattered.

When I reached home, my housemate was about to leave for work. He asked why I was home so early. I told him everything. He sat beside me quietly. There were no words that could help.

Soon after, my brother arrived. We booked our tickets and somehow managed to get a flight at 8:45 p.m. From that moment on, I didn't know what else to do except cry. Crying felt like the only thing my body still knew how to do.

I had always liked airports. They meant movement—journeys, reunions, the promise of coming back home. But that day, the airport became the worst place in the world for me.

My brother and I sat there together, side by side, holding each other's hands. We were both crying, yet not a single word came out of our mouths. There was nothing left to say. Words had lost their meaning.

We kept our heads down in that public place. Our eyes were filled with tears, and we did not have the courage to face the world.

Our world had already collapsed. In that moment, surrounded by people rushing to catch flights, we were standing still—broken, helpless, and suddenly orphaned of our strength

Back home, my family was discussing my father's cremation. I was furious. How could they even think about this when his two children were not there? I wasn't ready. I would never be ready.

It had been three years since I had last seen him. Three years of waiting, postponing, convincing myself that there would be another chance. I wanted to see him one last time—in person. I wanted my eyes to confirm what my heart was refusing to accept.

I had wanted to come home for so long, but for many reasons, I couldn't. Still, I never imagined that this would be how I would return. I had planned something else entirely—celebrations, time together, laughter, making up for lost moments.

But destiny had written a different ending for me.

But my brother explained something that broke me even more. He said that if they waited for us— my mother had to sit there all day and all night—she would fall sick. We would reach home only after 17–18 hours. She wouldn't survive that wait.

With a heart I didn't recognize as my own, I gave permission for my father's last rites to be performed.

I hated that decision. I still do. But now, we only have our mother. And the thought of losing her too was something I couldn't bear.

Some decisions are not choices.

They are sacrifices made in moments when you are already broken.

And that was the day my life divided itself into two parts—before 3rd December, and everything that came after.

Chapter 7

Reaching Home without Him

The journey back home felt endless. Time moved, but I didn't. My body was traveling, yet my heart was still stuck on that phone call—*"Dad is not responding."* Every passing hour took me farther from him and closer to a reality I wasn't ready to face.

When we finally reached home after those long 18-20 hours, the house didn't feel like home anymore. It felt unfamiliar, Heavy, Silent in a way that screamed. He wasn't there to receive us. No voice, No presence, No warmth.

That was when it truly hit me—I was too late.

People were everywhere, yet I felt completely alone. Everyone was speaking, crying, offering condolences, but none of it reached me. My eyes searched for him instinctively, even though my mind knew he wouldn't be there. Hope doesn't disappear immediately; it lingers painfully.

Seeing my mother broke me in a way nothing else could. She looked smaller, weaker, like someone whose strength had been quietly taken away. She didn't cry loudly. She just existed in silence, the same silence my father had carried all his life. In that moment, I understood where her strength had always come from —and how deeply she had loved him.

I wanted to scream. I wanted to collapse. But I couldn't. I became strong because I had to. Because she needed me. Because my father had raised me to stand when everything inside me wanted to fall apart.

Every corner of the house carried him. His belongings. His habits. His absence. The chair he sat on. The space he filled without effort. Losing him didn't feel like losing a person—it felt like losing stability itself.

That day, I learned a truth I will carry forever:

We don't grieve only the people we lose—we grieve the future we imagined with them. And with my dad, I had imagined so much. My plans with him were endless.

I used to tell him that when I came home, we would travel together. We would go to Jammu & Kashmir, then Vrindavan then Salasar Balaji. There were so many places living in my mind, waiting for us. I had pictured every journey, every moment, and every smile.

I wanted to buy things for him—not because he needed them, but because I wanted to choose them for him. New clothes, selected by me. Perfumes I thought would suit him. Watches he could wear proudly. I don't even know what else—just small ways of saying thank you, of giving back a fraction of what he gave us.

Now all those plans remain unfinished. They live only in my heart, where he still exists, listening, smiling, and letting me dream.

I had returned home, but I had arrived in a world that would never be the same again.

Chapter 8

The Love That Shaped Me

Every girl is close to her father, but with me, it was always a little more than that. He never called me his princess. Instead, he would smile and say, *"You are my second son."* And those were never just words. He lived by them. He raised me like one, trusted me like one, and stood beside me like one.

I never wore girly clothes. He bought shorts and shirts for me when I was young, and even when I was in college—when we attended weddings—he would still choose pants and shirts for me. Sometimes I would laugh and tease him, saying, *"Papa, I'm a big girl now. I should start wearing girly clothes."* He would look at me and simply say, *"You look good in these."* And that was the end of the conversation.

I never behaved like a typical girl, and he never tried to make me one. The confidence I carry today, the freedom I learned to hold responsibly, came from him. At that time, I didn't realize how rare that kind of trust was.

I had many male friends, yet he never doubted me—not even once. He never checked my phone, even though he knew I stayed awake late at night, busy scrolling or talking. If something ever crossed his mind, he didn't spy or control. He would either say directly, *"I don't like that,"* or gently ask, *"What's going on?"*

That was his way—quiet trust, clear boundaries, and a belief in me that never wavered.

Every night, sharp at 8:00p.m., I waited for him. The moment I heard the horn of his scooter, I would run out into the street to open the door for him. This wasn't just a childhood habit—it stayed with me until the day I moved to

Canada. No matter how old I grew, that part of me never changed.

I was stubborn. I always wanted to take my own decisions, and he never stopped me. Even when he knew I was making the wrong choice, he let me go ahead. Not because he didn't care— but because he wanted me to become strong and independent. He wanted me to be mature enough to understand right and wrong on my own, especially for the day when he wouldn't be there.

His love for me was unconditional. I still don't understand how he loved me so deeply. I fought with everyone. I talked back. I was difficult. Yet his love never changed. He forgave me every time. He never said the words *"I forgive you,"* but I always knew because he never stayed angry. His silence was his forgiveness.

I love him more than words can hold, and I am going to miss him more than my heart can understand. Every second, I will miss him. No one's love can ever replace his.

I never wanted him to leave us so early. Before going, he made sure we were settled—that we wouldn't have to worry about anything after he was gone. Even in his leaving, he was still protecting us.

When I was a child, I believed money could replace everything. As I grew older, I learned the true value of loved ones. Just when I was learning that parents should never be left alone, he left me.

He didn't even give me a chance to do something for him in his last days.

I want to cry endlessly, but I can't find a corner in my own house to cry. Because he still feels present. And somewhere inside me, I feel that if I cry, he would feel bad.

So I hold my tears the way he held his pain—silently.

Chapter 9

The People He Left Behind

When Papa passed away, people came in numbers I had never seen before. Our house was filled with relatives, neighbors, friends, colleagues—faces from different phases of his life. At first, I was overwhelmed. Then I was shocked.

I realized something that day.

He didn't gather so many people because of money, power, or status. He gathered them because of who he was-because of his behavior, his kindness, his honesty, and his brave heart. He lived a simple life, but he left behind a legacy richer than wealth.

Among all those faces, one sight shook me from within his best friend, my uncle, sitting in front of us and crying uncontrollably. Seeing him like that broke something inside me. They were not just friends; they were brothers by choice. They shared a bond deeper than blood.

They treated each other's children as their own. There was never a difference. No comparison. No boundaries. We grew up knowing that love doesn't always come from the same blood line

—it comes from the same heart.

A few days later, I spoke to my uncle. He said something that stayed with me forever:

"We don't get to choose our parents, our siblings, or our family by birth. But friends—that choice are ours."

And then he added, "I was lucky that your Papa and I found each other."

That moment made me realize how rare their bond was. How blessed they were to walk through life together.

As his children, we had each other. We could cry openly in front of relatives and friends. But I often wondered about my uncle— what he must be going through alone. He had lost his brother, his companion, his safe place.

He smiled for others. He spoke with strength. But behind that strength, I knew he was broken too—just like us.

Loss doesn't only belong to family. Sometimes, it belongs even more deeply to those who chose you.

Last page:-

Papa, this is everything I never got to say… Papa, My heart feels empty without you.

I never imagined a world where I couldn't hear your voice, where I couldn't call you and hear you ask,

"Chanu Beta, khana khaya?"

Those small words meant everything…and now they echo in my mind every day. There were so many moments when I wanted to say I'm sorry —sorry for the mistakes I made, sorry for not understanding things sooner, sorry for the times I was stubborn…

But Papa, I know you loved me beyond all of that.

You never showed anger — only love, only patience. You stood with me when no one else dared to.

In a world where people judge daughters, you protected me. You saved me.

You believed in me.

You sent me far away, not because you wanted distance—but because you wanted me to live, to be safe, and to have a future. Papa…I didn't know that our last meeting would truly be the last. If I had known, I would have hugged you longer.

I would have memorized your face more carefully. I would have told you how much you mean to me.

I would have told you that everything I am, everything I achieve, is because of the sacrifices you made for me. The guilt, the distances, the things left unsaid they hurt me every day.

But I know…

I know you left this world with love in your heart, not complaints. You were proud of me.

You wanted me to be strong, to survive, to live a life bigger than the pain of the past. Papa, I miss you. I miss you in a way that words can't hold.

I miss your smile, your voice, your quiet strength.

I miss the man who made my world safe. I hope you are somewhere peaceful, watching over me.

I hope you know that I carry you with me in everything I do.

I hope you feel my love reaching you, even from this world to the next. I love you, Papa. *More than I ever said.* More than this world will ever understand. And I'll love you for the rest of my life.

Author's Note

This book is my truth. It is not perfect, just like life. It is filled with emotions, flaws, love, and loss. If it moves you, comforts you, or reminds you of someone you love—then it has done its job.

Hold your people close. Time is never promised. Life is unscripted.